Principles of Costing
Wise Guide

AAT Level 2 Certificate in Accounting

© Aubrey Penning, 2022, 2024

All rights reserved. No part of this publication may be reproduced, stored in a retrieval system, or transmitted in any form or by any means, electronic, mechanical, photo-copying, recording or otherwise, without the prior consent of the copyright owners, or in accordance with the provisions of the Copyright, Designs and Patents Act 1988, or under the terms of any licence permitting limited copying issued by the Copyright Licensing Agency, Saffron House, 6-10 Kirby Street, London EC1N 8TS.

Image of owl © Eric Isselée-Fotolia.com

Published by Osborne Books Limited
Tel 01905 748071, Email books@osbornebooks.co.uk, Website www.osbornebooks.co.uk

Printed and bound by Stroma Ltd, UK.

ISBN 978-1-911198-86-4

how to use this Wise Guide

This Wise Guide has been designed to supplement your Tutorial and Workbook. It has two main aims:

- to reinforce your learning as you study your course
- to help you prepare for your online assessment

This Wise Guide is organised in the specific topic areas listed on pages 4 and 5. These individual topic areas have been designed to cover the main areas of study, concentrating on specific areas of difficulty. There is also an index at the back to help you find the areas you are studying or revising.

The Owl symbolises wisdom, and acts as your tutor, introducing and explaining topics. Please let us know if he is doing his job properly. If you have feedback on this material please email books@osbornebooks.co.uk.

Thank you and good luck with your study and revision.

Osborne Books

REVISION TIPS

*'OWL' stands for: **O**bserve **W**rite **L**earn*

There are a number of well-known ways in which you can remember information:

- *You can remember what it looks like on the page. Diagrams, lists, mind-maps, colour coding for different types of information, all help you **observe** and remember.*

- *You can remember what you **write** down. Flash cards, post-it notes around the bathroom mirror, notes on a mobile phone all help. It is the process of writing which helps to fix the information in the brain.*

- *You can **learn** by using this Wise Guide. Read through each topic carefully and then prepare your own written version on flash cards, post-it notes, wall charts – anything that you can see regularly.*

- *Lastly, give yourself **chill out** time, your brain a chance to recover and the information time to sink in. Promise yourself treats when you have finished studying – a drink, chocolate, a work out. Relax! And pass.*

list of contents

1	Introduction to costing	6
2	Elements of cost	8
3	Direct and indirect costs	12
4	Costs analysed by function	18
5	Revenue, cost, profit and investment centres; coding	22
6	Absorption of overheads	26
7	How costs behave	30
8	Calculations using cost behaviour	36
9	Inventory valuation	40
10	Managing materials inventory	56

11	Manufacturing accounts	58
12	Labour payments	64
13	Budgets and variances	68
14	Reporting	72
15	Calculation tools – spreadsheets	74
16	Memory aids	78
	Index	84

1 Introduction to costing

WHAT IS COSTING?

Costing involves working out the costs for an organisation such as a business.

These are the costs incurred by the business making products, or providing services.

the need for costing in an organisation

The costs are used within the organisation and they help the management to:

- set selling prices
- monitor and control expenditure
- plan for the future

Costs are usually worked out for a **unit** (eg one item of production), or **in total** for a number of units over a period of time.

management accounting and financial accounting

The 'Principles of Costing' that you study is part of the area of accounting called **management accounting**. The 'Bookkeeping' subjects you study are part of the other main area of accounting that is called **financial accounting**. The main differences are shown below:

MANAGEMENT ACCOUNTING	**FINANCIAL ACCOUNTING**
accounting data for INTERNAL use	accounting data for EXTERNAL use
used for FUTURE financial planning	reporting PAST financial performance
set out in budgets and forecasts	set out in formal financial statements
using detailed financial information	based on summaries of the accounts
in a format set by the organisation in line with INTERNAL requirements	in a format required by EXTERNAL rules and regulations

2 Elements of cost

Elements of cost

Costs can be divided up into 'elements' – in other words, categories of cost. There are three main elements of cost:
- *materials*
- *labour*
- *expenses (sometimes called 'overheads')*

the three elements of cost: materials, labour and expenses (overheads)

These can be defined as follows:

- **materials** are physical things that are used to make a product or to provide a service

- **labour** is the cost of paying people to make a product or provide a service

- **expenses** (sometimes referred to as 'overheads') refers to the costs of providing everything that isn't either material or labour

EXAMPLE: the three elements of cost

The three examples of businesses shown below all incur different types of cost, classified as materials, labour and expenses. It is probably easier to analyse costs into materials and labour first, and then everything else must be an expense!

the business	materials	labour	expenses
Double glazing manufacturer	glass, plastic, aluminium	assemblers' pay, office staff pay	factory lighting, office rent
Taxi service	fuel for taxis	taxi drivers' pay, receptionist's pay	taxi insurance, office heating
Hairdressing business	shampoo, conditioner	stylists' pay, trainees' pay	business rates, electricity

calculating the cost of one unit of output

You can calculate the total cost of producing **one unit** of output by adding together all the three elements of cost:

cost of one unit =

cost of **materials** to produce one unit

+ cost of **labour** to produce one unit

+ cost of **expenses** paid out for the production of one unit

EXAMPLE: working out the unit cost for Bluebeard Limited

Bluebeard Limited makes a single product. The cost details are as follows:

Materials: each unit uses 3 kilograms of material that costs £2.20 per kilogram

Labour: each unit takes 10 minutes of labour that costs £12.00 per hour

Expenses: the total expenses required to make 5,000 units is £18,000

Calculation: unit cost for Bluebeard Limited

The cost of each element to make one unit is calculated as shown below.
These amounts are then added together to arrive at a **total cost per unit**.

Element of Cost	Unit Cost £	Workings
Materials	6.60	3 kilos x £2.20 per kilo
Labour	2.00	£12.00 per hour x 10 minutes ÷ 60 (each unit takes 10 minutes to make and there are 60 minutes in an hour)
Expenses	3.60	£18,000 ÷ 5,000 units
Total cost of one unit	12.20	

3 Direct and indirect costs

Other classifications of cost

*There are other ways of classifying costs which this Wise Guide will explain – for example classification by **nature**. The term 'nature of cost' is used to describe costs as being either **direct** or **indirect**. This distinction describes **how closely the cost is related** to the product being made or the service being provided.*

direct and indirect costs (nature of costs)

- **direct costs** are costs that **can be identified** directly with each unit of output, for example the materials used in the manufacture of a product

- **indirect costs** are costs that **cannot be identified** directly with specific units of output, for example the insurance taken out by the manufacturer of a product

This classification of cost is illustrated in the example on the next page.

> ### EXAMPLE: distinguishing between direct and indirect costs
>
> Chipper Limited makes timber products including garden sheds, summer houses and fencing. If you take the example of manufacturing a garden shed, the cost details are as follows:
>
> **Direct cost**
> The cost of the timber used to make a garden shed is a **direct cost** – the timber can be clearly identified with the shed. It is possible to work out how much timber went into making the shed and then work out its materials cost.
>
> **Indirect cost**
> An example of an **indirect cost** is the cost of insurance for the factory where the sheds are made. This cost relates **indirectly** to all the sheds (and anything else) that are made in the factory. The business needs to incur this cost, but it cannot be directly linked to any particular shed, or any other product.

This classification of cost is linked on the next page to the 'materials, labour and expenses' classification.

materials, labour and expenses costs – direct or indirect?

- **MATERIALS costs** can be **direct** or **indirect**
  - **direct materials** are the materials that go into the manufacture of the product, eg flour, eggs and sugar are direct materials that are used to make cakes
  - **indirect materials** are more remote from the final product or service; for example lubrication oil for machinery that is used to manufacture products

- **LABOUR costs** can be **direct** or **indirect**
  - **direct labour** is the cost of employing people who are directly involved with making products (or providing services), eg assembly workers in a factory
  - **indirect labour** is the cost of employees who are a stage further away from the product or service, eg supervisors, managers and support staff

- **EXPENSES costs** are normally only **indirect**
  - **indirect expenses** normally relate to the organisation as a whole and are often referred to as **overheads**, eg electricity, insurance

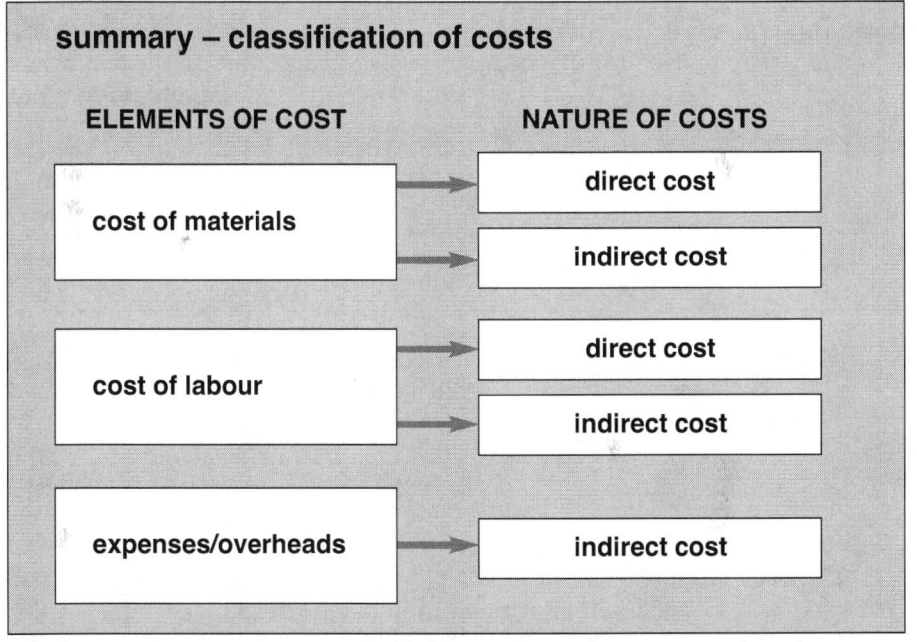

EXAMPLE: types of cost in a manufacturing business

Rollalong Ltd manufactures car tyres. The following table provides some examples of the types of cost incurred by Rollalong, and an analysis of the types of cost.

Rollalong Ltd – examples of costs		
	Direct	**Indirect**
Materials	Rubber to make tyres, Metal reinforcement	Lubricant for tyre manufacturing machinery, Office stationery
Labour	Manufacturing operatives' pay	Canteen staff pay, Factory supervisors' pay
Expenses	None	Electricity, Factory rent

formula to remember:
For a manufacturing organisation, the term **direct cost** is used to describe the total of the direct costs: **Direct materials + Direct labour = Direct cost (Prime cost)**

service providers – direct and indirect costs

It is important to remember that the distinction between direct and indirect costs also applies to **service providers**. Here is an analysis of costs incurred by a school.

EXAMPLE: types of cost in a service provider

Walford Road School – examples of costs		
	Direct	**Indirect**
Materials	Student textbooks, Student stationery	Cleaning materials, Office stationery
Labour	Teachers' pay	Office staff pay, Caretakers' pay
Expenses	None	Insurance, Internet access costs

reminder:
Note that all the examples of expenses are indirect costs. **Indirect expenses** are sometimes called **overheads**.

4 Costs analysed by function

Functional analysis

*As well as dividing costs up according to their elements and whether they are direct or indirect, we can also look at the separate parts of the organisation – the **functions** – where the costs are incurred. This is called **functional analysis**, and it builds on the analysis of costs that we have already seen.*

production and non-production costs

In a manufacturing business, the two main functions are production and non-production.

- **PRODUCTION** normally takes place in the factory; production costs can be:
  - **direct**, eg the cost of raw materials
  - **indirect**, eg the cost of factory heating

- **NON-PRODUCTION** occurs where support functions take place; the costs are **indirect** and cover areas such as administration, sales and distribution, finance

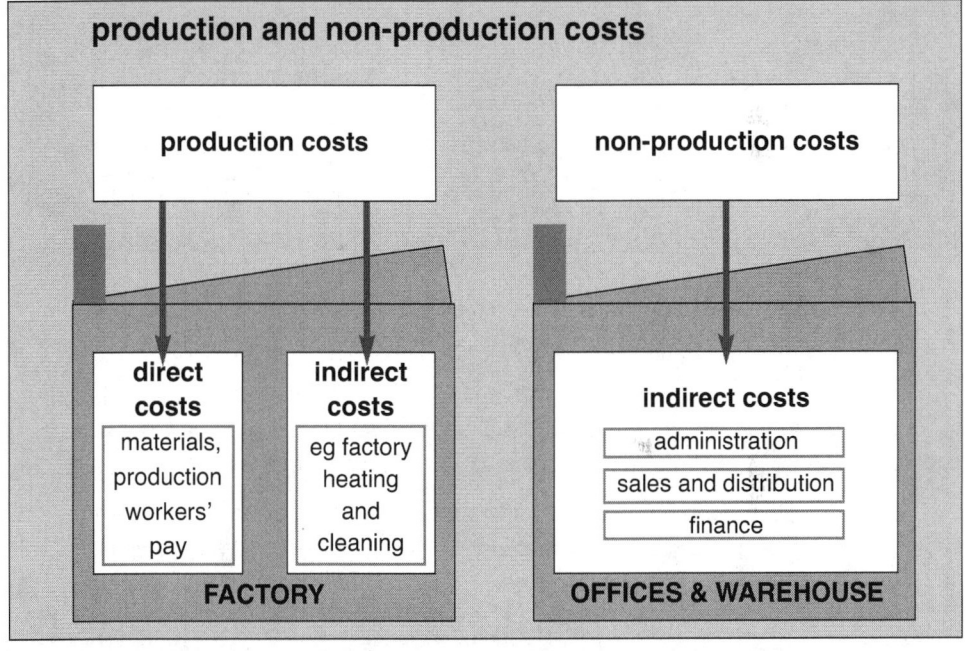

non-production costs – further notes

- **Administration** includes the costs incurred in running the organisation, for example the administrative costs of running the purchasing department, the human resources department (often called HR), the accounts office and the general office.

- **Sales and distribution** includes the costs of selling the products (eg sales reps' pay, marketing and advertising) and getting the products to the customers (eg warehouse and transport costs).

- **Finance** refers to the costs of using the money that is needed to run the organisation. Financial costs include interest payable on borrowing, and bank charges.

summary – the rules of costing for a manufacturing business

1. Production costs can be direct or indirect.
2. Non-production costs (administration, sales & distribution, and finance) are always indirect.
3. Materials and labour costs can be direct or indirect.
4. Expenses are nearly always indirect.

EXAMPLE: analysis of the costs of Rollalong Ltd, tyre manufacturer

	Production costs		Non-production costs		
	Direct production costs	*Indirect production costs*	*Indirect administration costs*	*Indirect sales and distribution costs*	*Indirect finance costs*
Materials	rubber, metal	lubricant for machinery	office stationery	fuel for delivery vehicles	
Labour	manufacturing operatives' pay	factory supervisors' pay	office staff pay	storekeepers' pay, sales reps' pay	
Expenses		factory rent, factory power	insurance of office	advertising costs, promotional events	interest, bank charges

5 Revenue, cost, profit and investment centres; coding

analysing costs

It is important for management to monitor the costs of various areas of an organisation and also to analyse the profitability of the different departments of the organisation.

*This is done by identifying appropriate **cost centres**, **profit centres** and **investment centres** and allocating amounts to those centres using **coding systems**.*

coding systems

- A coding system is the use of a series of numbers and/or letters to identify data.

- Common examples in everyday life are car registration plates (as you will discover if you have been zapped by a speed camera), postcodes and National Insurance numbers.

- Common examples in business are stock codes and **cost classification codes**.

revenue centres, cost centres, profit centres and investment centres

- **Revenue centres** are sections of a business to which income can be identified – they are only concerned with revenue, not costs.
- **Cost centres** are the areas of the organisation – eg functions or departments – which management need to monitor to see how much they **cost** to run.
- **Profit centres** work on the same principle as cost centres, but can collect income as well as costs – and work out the **profit** for that part of the business.
- **Investment centres** collect income and costs (like profit centres) but also record investment in that part of the business – and so can compare the **profit** with the amount **invested**.

COST CENTRES	PROFIT CENTRES	INVESTMENT CENTRES
an assembly section in a factory	a car showroom where cars are sold	one shop in a chain of shops
a goods despatch department	a restaurant in a hotel	a separate factory
a ward in a hospital	beauty treatment room in a leisure centre	an oil drilling platform

- **Revenue, cost, profit and investment centres** can be allocated data using **coding**.

EXAMPLE: using a coding system for income and costs

The Walford Bistro is a restaurant which uses the following numeric coding system:

Revenue / Profit / Cost Centre	Code	Sub-classification	Sub-code
Sales (revenue)	500	Restaurant sales	70
		Bar sales	80
		Take-away sales	90
Restaurant costs	100	Direct costs	10
		Indirect costs	20
Bar costs	200	Direct costs	10
		Indirect costs	20
Take-away costs	300	Direct costs	10
		Indirect costs	20

These examples of costs will be coded as follows:

- **Income** from selling take-away meals: 500/90
- **Cost** of licence needed to operate the bar: 200/20
- **Cost** of employing restaurant chef: 100/10
- **Cost** of buying take-away food containers: 300/10

these sub-codes subdivide the costs into direct and indirect costs

EXAMPLE: using a coding system for elements of cost

Rollalong Ltd, a tyre manufacturer, uses an alpha-numeric coding system for its costs, which are analysed by element (materials, labour and expenses) and also by whether they are direct or indirect costs.

Cost element	Code	Cost nature	Sub-code
Materials	M	Direct	20
		Indirect	50
Labour	L	Direct	20
		Indirect	50
Expenses (overheads)	E	Direct	20
		Indirect	50

These examples of costs will be coded as follows:

- Factory heating — E50
- Purchase of rubber to make tyres — M20
- Supervisors' pay — L50
- Promotional event at motor race — E50

6 Absorption of overheads

Under 'absorption costing', the indirect production costs (production overheads) of an organisation are added together and then are spread over the units of output (the items that are made). Indirect costs cannot be identified directly with each unit of output, so a way must be found of sharing out these costs so that the cost of each item made includes a fair amount of overhead cost.

There are three methods of absorbing production overheads that we need to be able to use. They all use budgeted data to calculate an 'overhead absorption rate' (OAR) which is then applied to each unit of product (or service). The methods are:

- **units of output method**
- **direct labour hours method**
- **machine hours method**

We will now see how each method works.

Units of output method

This method is only really suitable for situations where all the products made are the same or similar. This is because it absorbs the same amount of overhead onto each item.

The overhead absorption rate is calculated as:

$$\frac{\text{Budgeted overheads}}{\text{Budgeted units of output}} = \text{Absorption rate per unit}$$

For example, if a desk manufacturer had budgeted production overheads of £200,000 for next year, and budgeted output of 5,000 desks, the overhead absorption rate would be:

£200,000 ÷ 5,000 = £40 per desk.

If the direct costs for each desk were materials £30, and labour £45, then the total absorbed cost of each desk would be:

£30 + £45 + £40 = £115 per desk.

direct labour hours method

This method is useful when a range of different products are made in a labour intensive way. The absorption rate is calculated for each labour hour used, and this can then be applied to various products based on the budgeted labour hours per unit.

The overhead absorption rate is calculated as:

$$\frac{\text{Budgeted overheads}}{\text{Budgeted direct labour hours}} = \text{Absorption rate per direct labour hour}$$

For example, if an office furniture manufacturer had budgeted production overheads of £200,000 for next year, using 10,000 budgeted labour hours, the overhead absorption rate would be:

£200,000 ÷ 10,000 labour hours = £20 per direct labour hour.

If the direct costs for each desk were materials £30, and 3 hours of labour costing £45, then the total absorbed cost of each desk would be:

£30 + £45 + (3 x £20) = £135 per desk.

machine hours method

This method is useful when a range of different products are made in a machine intensive factory. The absorption rate is calculated for each machine hour used, and this can then be applied to various products based on the budgeted machine hours per unit.

The overhead absorption rate is calculated as:

$$\frac{\text{Budgeted overheads}}{\text{Budgeted machine hours}} = \text{Absorption rate per machine hour}$$

For example, if an office furniture manufacturer had budgeted production overheads of £200,000 for next year, using 8,000 budgeted machine hours, the overhead absorption rate would be:

£200,000 ÷ 8,000 machine hours = £25 per machine hour.

If each desk took 2 machine hours, and the direct costs were materials £30, and labour £45, then the total absorbed cost of each desk would be:

£30 + £45 + (2 x £25) = £125 per desk.

7 How costs behave

What is cost behaviour?

Cost behaviour is what happens to costs when the level of output changes – eg the number of tyres made or meals provided. There are three types of cost behaviour that you need to know about. The name for each cost behaviour is based on what happens to the total of the cost when the level of output changes.

the three types of cost behaviour

- **fixed costs** (and stepped costs) are costs where the total stays the same when the output changes within a range of activity

- **variable costs** are costs whose total changes in proportion to the output (for example the cost doubles when the output doubles)

- **semi-variable costs** are those that have part of the cost behaving as a fixed cost, and part of the cost behaving as a variable cost (ie a mix of the two)

fixed cost behaviour

- **Fixed costs** do not vary when the level of output or activity changes, within a range, but may 'step up' to a different amount outside the range (stepped costs).
- **Examples of fixed costs** include rent on premises, insurance, and any cost that does not vary with the level of output.
- **Fixed costs per unit** = fixed costs ÷ number of units produced.

EXAMPLE: payment of factory rent of £40 a day – a fixed cost.
Note that the fixed cost remains the same but the fixed cost **per unit** falls as production is increased.

output = 2 units per day	output = 4 units per day
total fixed cost = £40 per day	total fixed cost = £40 per day
fixed cost per unit = £20 per day	fixed cost per unit = £10 per day

variable cost behaviour

- **Variable costs** change when the level of output or activity changes; it costs more to produce more items and it costs less to produce fewer items.

- **Examples of variable costs** include materials and some labour costs on the production line, eg piecework (payment based on the number of items produced).

EXAMPLE: variable costs = £10 per unit
Note that the variable cost remains the same **per unit** but the overall cost increases in the same proportion as the increase in production.

output = 2 units per day	output = 4 units per day
variable cost per unit = £10	variable cost per unit = £10
total variable cost = £20 per day	total variable cost = £40 per day

semi-variable cost behaviour

Semi-variable costs include both **fixed costs and variable costs**.
When output increases, part of the total cost will remain the same (the fixed cost element) and the variable part of the cost will increase in line with production.
Semi-variable costs therefore **increase with production, but not at the same rate**.

EXAMPLE:

output = 2 units per day		output = 4 units per day	
Semi-variable cost	£60	Semi-variable cost	£80
semi-variable cost per unit:		**semi-variable cost per unit:**	
£60 ÷ 2 (units) =	£30	£80 ÷ 4 (units) =	£20

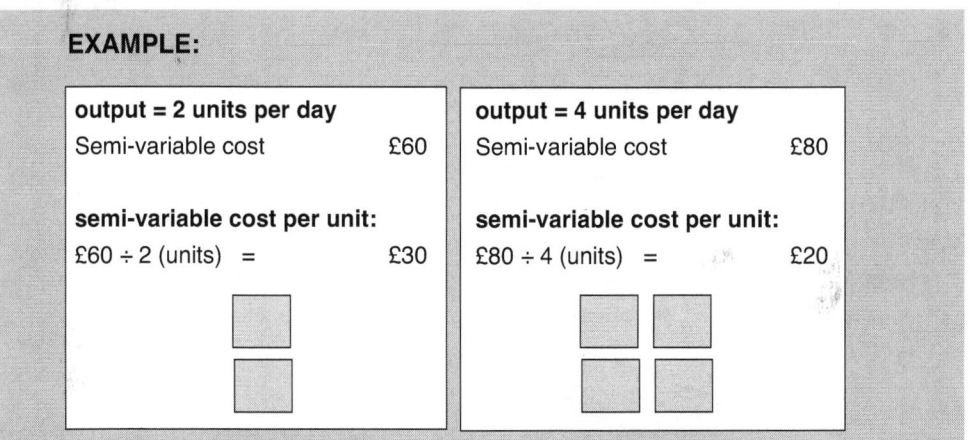

key points of cost behaviour

- A **fixed cost** is a cost that stays the same when output increases or decreases within a range, eg the cost of renting a factory.
- A **variable cost** is a cost, **the total of which changes in proportion to the output**, eg the materials cost of production: the **cost per unit for a variable cost will not change with the number made**.
- A **semi-variable cost** is fixed cost plus variable cost; it increases with the output, **but not at the same rate (proportion)** as the output.

EXAMPLE: how cost behaviour works in practice

What will happen if the number of items made in a period **doubles**?

- if the **total** of the specific cost (eg rent) does **not change**, it is a **fixed cost**
- if the **total** of the specific cost (eg materials) **doubles**, it is a **variable cost**
- if the **total** of the specific cost goes up, but **not as much as double** (eg the cost of power containing a fixed element), it is a **semi-variable cost**

cost behaviour – a summary

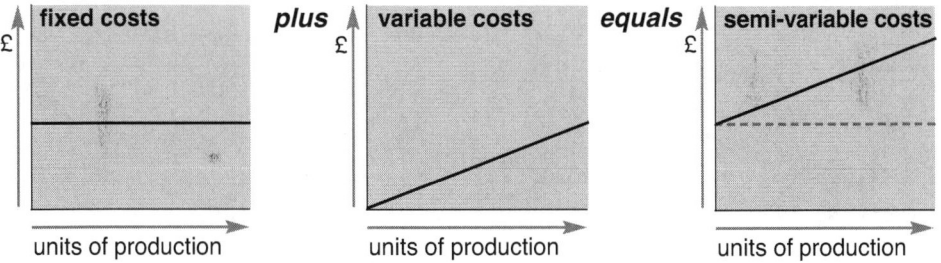

and some examples ...		
fixed costs	**variable costs**	**semi-variable costs**
labour paid on the basis of a fixed weekly wage	labour paid on the basis of items produced (piecework)	flat rate labour plus production bonus
standing charge for power supply in factory	charge per unit of power used by factory	total power bill for factory

8 Calculations using cost behaviour

Because of the straightforward way in which variable costs and fixed costs operate, we can carry out calculations to work out total costs. All we need to know is:
- *the fixed cost*
- *the variable cost per unit*

We will then be able to work out the costs at various levels of output.

EXAMPLE – calculation of unit cost

Suppose we are given the following data:

- the fixed costs in total are £48,000

- variable costs are £15 per unit

We can then work out all the costs that we need, using the table on the next page.

calculation of unit cost

Units	Fixed costs £	Variable costs £	Total costs £	Unit cost £
3,000	48,000	45,000	93,000	31
4,000	48,000	60,000	108,000	27

- number of units
- costs fixed at £48,000
- number of units x variable cost of £15
- fixed costs of £48,000 + variable costs
- total costs ÷ number of units

comment:
The unit cost **falls** as the total number of units **rises**, but not in the same proportion. This is because the fixed costs are shared among more units.

calculations involving more than one variable cost

It is also straightforward to work out the total cost per unit if you are given more than one variable cost. In the following example there are two variable costs – materials and labour.

EXAMPLE: calculating cost per unit using two variable costs

A company makes a single product and has **fixed costs** of £125,000.
Variable costs per unit are:
- materials: £600 per 50 units
- labour: £16 per hour (each unit takes 15 minutes to make)

The following table of costs is based on the production of 25,000 units.

Costs	Total cost £	Total cost workings	Unit cost £	Unit cost workings
Materials	300,000	£600 x 25,000 ÷ 50	12	£300,000 ÷ 25,000
Labour	100,000	£16 x 25,000 ÷ 60/15	4	£100,000 ÷ 25,000
Fixed costs	125,000	Fixed at £125,000	5	£125,000 ÷ 25,000
Total	525,000		21	£525,000 ÷ 25,000 (or, £12 + £4 + £5)

another calculation of unit cost

Another type of task could involve the cost data being provided in the following format:

EXAMPLE: calculating the unit costs

A company that makes a single product provides the following cost data for a production level of 20,000 units:

- **Materials**: 80,000 kilos at £4 per kilo
- **Labour**: 5,000 hours at £12 per hour
- **Fixed costs**: £180,000

The task just requires the calculation of the unit costs. The working set out below is provided so that you can see how it is calculated.

	Unit cost £	*Unit cost workings*
Materials	16	*80,000 x £4 ÷ 20,000*
Labour	3	*5,000 x 12 ÷ 20,000*
Fixed costs	9	*£180,000 ÷ 20,000*
Total unit cost	28	

9 Inventory valuation

the importance of valuing inventory
It is important for a manufacturing business to know the value of its inventory – ie the materials it purchases in order to manufacture a product. This is so that it can work out the profit that it is making on its products.

the manufacturing process

The manufacturing process involves **three** distinct stages: buying the inventory, storing the inventory and then issuing it out of storage for use in production by the business.

valuation of inventory – a problem and three solutions

- Valuation would be simple if the materials (inventory) purchased by a business over time were bought at the same price. All inventory would then have the same value.

- The **problem** is that the **prices paid** for materials will inevitably **change over time** and inventory held in storage may well have been **bought at different prices.**

- The valuation of inventory matters because when purchase prices vary we need to have a system that tells us how to value **the issues from the store** (the inventory used in production) and value of **what is left in the store**.

- There are **three ways of valuing inventory**. A business would normally need to pick one method and then stick to it. The method chosen is for **valuation purposes only** – it doesn't have to keep track of individual deliveries of materials. The three methods of valuation are known by their initial letters:

    - **FIFO**   **F**irst **I**n, **F**irst **O**ut
    - **LIFO**   **L**ast **I**n, **F**irst **O**ut
    - **AVCO**   **AV**erage **CO**st

We will now see how all these work, using simple examples to illustrate the methods.

FIFO – First In First Out

- This method means that **for valuation purposes** the first inventory you issue to production is the inventory that you have held the longest in the stores.

- The inventory left in the stores after the issue to production **will be valued at the latest purchase prices**.

- The figures used for valuation relate to the **purchase prices paid** and the **date order** of these purchases – they do **not** relate to specific items of inventory.

The example below illustrates FIFO in action.

> **FIFO EXAMPLE (see next page for diagram)**
>
> There are six units of inventory held in storage with the valuations marked on them.
>
> The dates of purchase are shown, the earliest on the left and the latest on the right.
>
> On May 6 three units are issued out of stores to production.
>
> They are the first to be purchased (on May 1 - May 3), hence 'First In, First Out.'
>
> The three units purchased last (May 4 - May 6) are left in the stores.

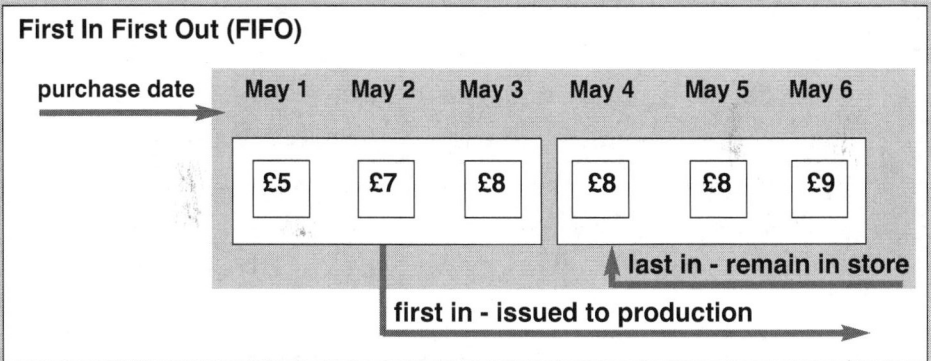

- The three units issued to production using FIFO are valued at:
  £5 + £7 + £8 = £20
- The three units left in the stores are valued at £8 + £8 + £9 = £25
- The total value of the issues to production plus the value of the inventory left in storage is £20 + £25 = £45. As you will see, this total value will be the same whatever inventory valuation method is used – FIFO, LIFO or AVCO.

LIFO – Last In First Out

- This method means that **for valuation purposes** the first inventory you issue to production is the **last** inventory that you have received into the stores.
- The inventory left in the stores **will be valued at the earliest purchase prices**.
- The figures used for valuation relate to the **purchase prices paid** and the **date order** in which these prices were paid – they do **not** relate to items of inventory.

The example below illustrates LIFO in action.

> **LIFO EXAMPLE (see next page for diagram)**
>
> There are six units of inventory held in storage with the valuations marked on them.
>
> The dates of purchase are shown, the earliest on the left and the latest on the right.
>
> On May 6 three units are issued out of stores to production.
>
> They are the **last** to be purchased (on May 4 - May 6), hence 'Last In, First Out.'
>
> The three units purchased **first** (May 1- May 3) are left in the stores.

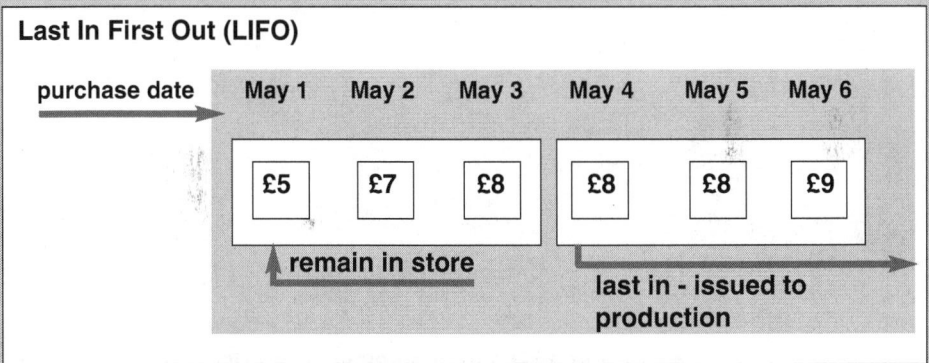

- The three units issued to production using LIFO are valued at:
  £8 + £8 + £9 = £25.
- The three units left in the stores are valued at £5 + £7 + £8 = £20.
- The total value of the issues to production plus the value of the inventory left in storage is £25 + £20 = £45. As you will see, this total value will be the same whatever inventory valuation method is used – LIFO, FIFO or AVCO.

AVCO – Average Cost (weighted average)

- This method of valuation is completely different from LIFO or FIFO because the valuation of inventory is the **average cost of the purchases** held in the stores.

- As a result, all the inventory is **valued at the same price**. The formula used is:

  average cost per unit of inventory = $\dfrac{\text{total cost of inventory in the stores}}{\text{number of units in the stores}}$

- This average is always **recalculated after each purchase**.

> **AVCO EXAMPLE** (see next page for diagram)
>
> There are six units of inventory held in storage; the purchase prices are shown on the diagram. The date of purchase is not shown – it is not used in the calculation.
>
> The average unit cost is worked out at $\dfrac{£5 + £7 + £8 + £8 + £8 + £9}{6 \text{ (units)}}$ = £7.50 per unit
>
> On May 6 three units **valued at £7.50** each are issued out of stores to production.
>
> On May 6 three units **valued at £7.50** each are left in the stores.

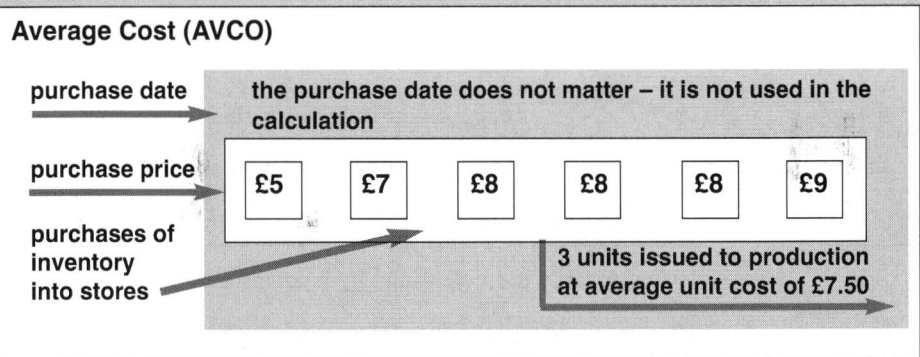

- The total value of the issue to production using AVCO is £7.50 x 3 = £22.50.
- The three units left in the stores are also valued at £7.50 until further purchases are made. This value is £7.50 x 3 = £22.50.
- The total value of the issues to production plus the value of the inventory left in storage is £22.50 + £22.50 = £45, ie the same total produced by the LIFO and FIFO methods of valuation.

features of inventory valuation

You need to remember the features of the three valuation methods: FIFO, LIFO and AVCO. These are set out in the table below.

	FIFO	LIFO	AVCO
VALUATION OF ISSUES OF INVENTORY TO PRODUCTION			
Issues of inventory are valued at the **oldest purchase prices**	✓		
Issues of inventory are valued at the **most recent purchase prices**		✓	
Issues of inventory are valued at the **average cost of purchases**			✓
VALUATION OF INVENTORY LEFT IN THE STORES			
Inventory is valued at the **most recent purchase price**	✓		
Inventory is valued at the **oldest purchase price**		✓	
Inventory is valued at the **average cost of purchases**			✓

the effects of price changes on inventory valuations

The three methods of stock valuation – FIFO, LIFO and AVCO – will produce different valuation results as inventory prices rise and fall. This is shown in the following table.

	FIFO	LIFO	AVCO
WHAT HAPPENS WHEN INVENTORY COSTS RISE?			
lower issue costs but higher balance left in stores valuations	✓		
higher issue costs but lower balance left in stores valuations		✓	
the same valuation for issues and the balance left in stores			✓
WHAT HAPPENS WHEN INVENTORY COSTS FALL?			
higher issue costs but lower balance valuations	✓		
lower issue costs but higher balance valuations		✓	
the same valuation for issues and the balance left in stores			✓

inventory valuation using a table which records receipts and issues

We will now use a table of data recording inventory receipts and issues to work out the valuation of inventory. We will again use the three methods: FIFO, LIFO and AVCO.

EXAMPLE: INVENTORY VALUATION USING FIFO (FIRST IN, FIRST OUT)

The table below shows the receipts of inventory into stores and issues to production during the month of March. A valuation of the issues to production and remaining balance in stores is required for March 30. The calculations are on the next page.

Date	Receipts		Issues
	Units	Cost (£)	Units
March 16	100	600	
March 19	250	850	
March 26	200	750	
March 28			150
March 30	400	1,800	

Calculation of the inventory values using FIFO

- The issue of 150 units into production will be valued at the **earliest cost price**.
- In this case this will involve valuations of two deliveries into the stores: the 100 units received on March 16, and 50 out of the 250 units purchased on March 19.
- The **valuation of the issue** is calculated as follows:

March 16 (100 units)	£600
March 19 (50 units @ £850/250)	£170
Total valuation of issue of 150 units =	£770

- The **balance of inventory held in the stores on March 30** is as follows:

200 units received on March 19 ([250 – 50] @ £850/250)	£680
200 units received on March 26	£750
400 units received on March 30	£1,800
Total valuation of all units left in stores at March 30	£3,230

- A **useful check** here is to add the issues valuation (£770) to the balance (£3,230); this will equal the total cost of the receipts (£4,000).

EXAMPLE: INVENTORY VALUATION USING LIFO (LAST IN, FIRST OUT)

We will now repeat the valuation calculations, using the same data in the table below, **using the LIFO (Last In First Out) method**. Remember that issues to production using this method are valued at the cost of the **latest purchase(s)**.

Again, the valuations will be as at 30 March. The calculations are on the next page.

Date	Receipts		Issues
	Units	Cost (£)	Units
March 16	100	600	
March 19	250	850	
March 26	200	750	
March 28			150
March 30	400	1,800	

Calculation of the inventory values using LIFO

- The issue of 150 units into production is valued at the **latest purchase price**.

- This will involve the valuation of the delivery of 200 units into the stores on March 26.

- The **valuation of the issue of 150 units** is calculated as follows:
  March 26 (150 out of 200 units): $\frac{£750}{200} \times 150$ = £562.50

- The **balance of inventory held in the stores on March 30** is as follows:

100 units received on March 16	£600.00
250 units received on March 19	£850.00
50 of the 200 units received on March 26 ([200–150] @ $\frac{£750}{200}$)	£187.50
400 units received on March 30 (arrived after issue)	£1,800.00
Total valuation of all the units left in storage at March 30	£3,437.50

- A **useful check** here is to add the issues valuation (£562.50) to the balance (£3,437.50); this will equal the total of the receipts (£4,000).

EXAMPLE:
INVENTORY VALUATION USING AVCO (AVERAGE COST)

We will now repeat the valuation calculations, using the same data in the table below, **using the AVCO (Average cost) method**. Remember that this method completely ignores the date order of the inventory deliveries and takes a simple average of the valuations of all the inventory held in the store at the date of issue.

Date	Receipts		Issues
	Units	**Cost (£)**	**Units**
March 16	100	600	
March 19	250	850	
March 26	200	750	
March 28			150
March 30	400	1,800	

- To value the issue of 150 units into production on March 28 we must first work out the weighted average cost per unit of the receipts **up to that date**.

- To get the weighted **average cost per unit** we divide the total cost of the receipts up to March 28 by the total units. The calculation is:

$$\frac{£600 + £850 + £750}{100 + 250 + 200 \text{ units}} = \frac{£2,200}{550 \text{ units}} = £4.00 \text{ per unit}$$

This means that all the units of inventory held on March 28 will be valued at £4.

- The **valuation of the issue of 150 units** on March 28 will therefore be:
    150 units x £4 = £600

- The **balance of inventory held in the stores on March 28** will be:
    400 units x £4 = £1,600

- The receipt of 400 units on March 30 means that a new average cost per unit must be calculated as follows:

$$\frac{£1,600 + £1,800}{400 + 400 \text{ units}} = \frac{£3,400}{800 \text{ units}} = £4.25 \text{ per unit}$$

- If no further inventory is received, the next issue will be valued at £4.25 per unit.

Remember: the weighted average is recalculated after each receipt.

10 Managing materials inventory

why control inventory levels?
Organisations need to make sure that they hold an appropriate level of inventory of the various materials that they need. If they hold too much, they risk storage and cash flow problems; too little and they may run out and bring production to a halt.

inventory control policy

An organisation's inventory control policy will be used to manage inventory levels, and may refer to the following terms and state the various planned quantities and times:

- **buffer stock (inventory buffer)** – the amount of inventory that is held as a contingency – in case things don't go according to plan

- **lead time** – the length of time between placing an order for more material and it actually arriving

- **re-order level** – when the inventory level drops to the re-order level, it's time to place an order for more material

- **re-order quantity** – the quantity of material that should be ordered at a time (don't confuse this with re-order level!)

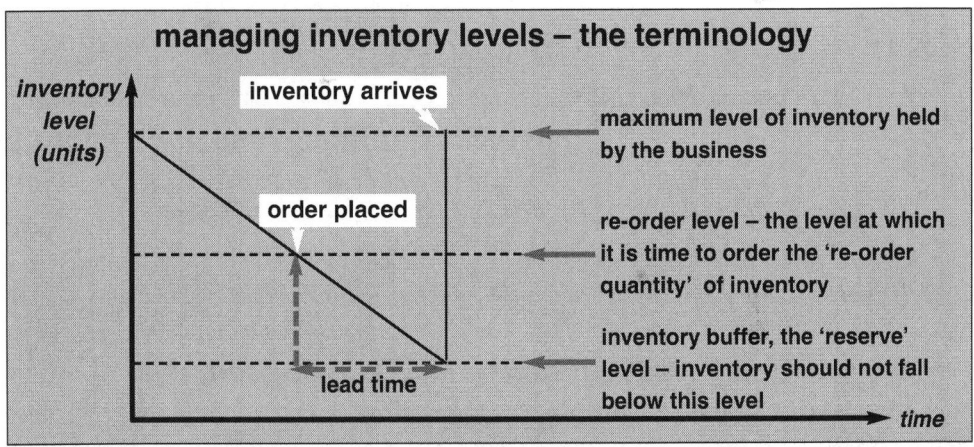

11 Manufacturing accounts

the function of a manufacturing account

Manufacturing accounts show how costs are built up over a specific period of time. Many of the names for costs you will already know. The bottom line of a manufacturing account shows the total manufacturing cost of the goods that have been sold. It is an important figure for the calculation of profit.

structure of a manufacturing account

These are the main calculations carried out in a manufacturing account:

	direct materials used
plus	direct labour
plus	manufacturing overheads
plus or *minus*	adjustment for work in progress
plus or *minus*	adjustment for finished goods *equals* **cost of goods sold**

This diagram shows the **subtotals** (in **CAPITALS**) that are produced as the manufacturing account is constructed.

The subtotals and their workings will be fully explained on the next few pages.

DIRECT MATERIALS USED + direct labour =	total direct costs: **DIRECT COST**	this is total direct costs plus the overheads paid in the manufacturing process	this is total direct costs plus the overheads paid in manufacturing, and adjusted for work-in progress (unfinished items) at the beginning and end of the accounting period	this is the total cost of manufacture, adjusted for finished items at the beginning and end of the accounting period
+ manufacturing overheads =		➤ **MANUFACTURING COST**		
+/– adjustment for work in progress =			➤ **COST OF GOODS MANUFACTURED**	
+/– adjustment for finished goods =				➤ **COST OF GOODS SOLD**

principles of costing wise guide – manufacturing accounts

explanation of the manufacturing account

We will now explain how each section of the manufacturing account is calculated.

It is probably a good idea to refer back to the diagram on the previous page to see how each section fits into the process and what each subtotal includes and means.

- **Direct materials used** are made up of:
    Opening inventory of raw materials (materials in the warehouse at the beginning of the accounting period)
  - \+ Purchases of raw materials
  - − Closing inventory of raw materials (materials in the warehouse at the end of the accounting period)
  - = **DIRECT MATERIALS USED**

- **Direct labour** is made up of the total cost of wages paid to production workers.

- **Direct cost** is a sub-total made up of
  Direct materials used
  - \+ Direct labour
  - = **DIRECT COST** – this is **the total direct costs of manufacture**

- **Manufacturing overheads** are indirect production costs, and are inserted without any adjustment. Factory rent is an example of a manufacturing overhead.

  Manufacturing cost is the next sub-total, calculated as follows:

  DIRECT COST
  - + Manufacturing overheads
  - = **MANUFACTURING COST**

- **Adjustment for work in progress** is the next stage:

  MANUFACTURING COST
  - + Opening inventory of work in progress (unfinished items in the factory at the beginning of the period)
  - − Closing inventory of work in progress (unfinished items in the factory at the end of the period)
  - = **COST OF GOODS MANUFACTURED**

- Adjustment for finished goods is the final stage in the process and results in the **Cost of Goods Sold**.

    This stage is calculated as follows:

    COST OF GOODS MANUFACTURED

    - + Opening inventory of finished goods (in the warehouse at the beginning of the period)
    - − Closing inventory of finished goods (in the warehouse at the end of the period)
    - = **COST OF GOODS SOLD**

completed manufacturing account

Set out on the next page is a completed manufacturing account with sample figures so that you can see how it all fits together.

Notice in particular which items are added and which are deducted. Plus and minus signs have been included here for clarity. In practice these would not appear on the account.

EXAMPLE: Manufacturing account

Opening inventory of raw materials	£15,000
Purchases of raw materials	+ £73,000
Closing inventory of raw materials	– £11,000
DIRECT MATERIALS USED	£77,000
Direct Labour	+ £45,000
DIRECT COST (PRIME COST)	£122,000
Manufacturing overheads	+ £113,000
MANUFACTURING COST	£235,000
Opening inventory of work in progress	+ £40,000
Closing inventory of work in progress	– £57,000
COST OF GOODS MANUFACTURED	£218,000
Opening inventory of finished goods	+ £78,000
Closing inventory of finished goods	– £70,000
COST OF GOODS SOLD	£226,000

12 Labour payments

labour payments and costing

We saw previously that labour is one of the elements of cost, and that there are both direct and indirect labour costs.

We also saw that labour costs can behave as fixed costs, variable costs or semi-variable costs depending on the method of calculation and payment.

We are now going to look in more detail at how labour payments are calculated. We will also explain the implications (including cost behaviour) of using these payment methods.

methods of calculating pay

There are four main methods of calculating pay that you will need to know:

- **time rate** – pay based on the actual hours worked, often known as 'basic pay'
- **overtime rate** – pay based on extra hours worked in addition to basic pay
- **bonus payments** – extra payments normally based on performance and productivity
- **piecework** – pay based on the number of items produced by the employee

We will now explain each of these payment methods in turn.

time rate with overtime

The following example shows how time rate works in practice and how overtime may be added on when an employee works additional hours.

S Singh and **V Duggan** are paid £12.00 per hour for work up to 38 hours per week. Any hours worked in excess of this are paid at £18.00 per hour (an overtime premium of £6.00 per hour).

We will calculate the gross wages for each employee (gross wage is the basic wage plus the payment for overtime).

Employee	Hours worked	Basic wage	Overtime	Gross wage
S Singh	36	36 hours x £12 = £432.00	£0.00	£432.00
V Duggan	40	38 hours x £12 = £456.00	(40 – 38 hours) x £18 = £36.00	£492.00

time rate with bonus

The following example shows how time rate works in practice and how a bonus payment may be added on when required.

> **N Smith** and **P Green** are paid £11.00 per hour for all hours worked. They are expected to produce 5 units per hour. If they produce more units than this they are paid a bonus of £2.50 per additional unit. Note that there is no bonus or deduction if the number of units produced is fewer than the expected number.

Employee	Hours worked	Units produced	Basic wage	Bonus	Gross wage
N Smith	38	196	38 hours x £11 = £418.00	(196 – [38 hrs x 5]) x £2.50 = £15.00	£433.00
P Green	42	200	42 hours x £11 = £462.00	(200 – [42 hours x 5]) x £2.50 = £0.00	£462.00

Note that P Green does not get a bonus because he has not produced enough items – he has worked 42 hours and should have produced 210 items in that time.

piecework

The calculation is based solely on the units produced. The time worked is not relevant.

S Holmes and **Q Moriarty** are paid £50.00 for every 4 units produced.

Employee	Hours worked	Units produced	Gross wage
S Holmes	38	48	(48 units ÷ 4) x £50 = £600
Q Moriarty	40	44	(44 units ÷ 4) x £50 = £550

implications and cost behaviour

	implications	cost behaviour
time rate	easy to operate, payment not based on output, no incentive to produce more	normally considered a fixed cost - not linked to output
time rate + bonus	guaranteed minimum pay for hours worked, incentive to produce more	semi-variable cost (the bonus is the variable element)
piecework	based on output and not time spent, possible fall in quality of work	a variable cost (it varies with output)

13 Budgets and variances

purpose of a budget

A budget is a financial plan, prepared in advance. It usually includes details of expected income and costs for the relevant period, broken down into suitable categories. It is initially used for planning purposes. Once the period has started, the actual amounts can be compared with the figures in the budget. This enables the budget to be used to monitor and control income and costs.

budgets and variances

- **Variances** measure the difference between budgeted and actual performance.
- Where the actual figures are **better than the budget** (eg the actual cost is lower or income is higher) variances are '**favourable**' (often abbreviated to 'FAV' or 'F').
- Where the actual figures are **worse than the budget** (eg the actual cost is higher or income is lower) variances are '**adverse**' (often abbreviated to 'ADV' or 'A').
- **Variances** are calculated from a table known as a **performance report**.

EXAMPLE: performance report

A business has produced a performance report for the last month. It sets out budgeted and actual income and costs in a table and has calculated the variances. It shows whether each variance is adverse or favourable.

	Budget £	Actual £	Variance £	Adverse	Favourable
Income	200,000	198,500	1,500	✔	
Direct materials	25,300	24,900	400		✔
Direct labour	48,600	49,700	1,100	✔	
Production overheads	71,400	72,000	600	✔	
Administration overheads	23,200	22,900	300		✔
Selling and distribution overheads	15,900	17,000	1,100	✔	

significant variances

- The main reason for monitoring variances is so that a business can identify **significant** areas which need **reporting to management** so that action can be taken if required.
- Most variances will not require any action to be taken, but if the variance is greater than a certain percentage set by the business of the budgeted amount (eg 3%), the variance becomes a **significant variance** and will need reporting to management.
- Both adverse and favourable variances can be significant.

calculation of significant variances

The percentage variance is calculated by dividing the variance by the budgeted amount and multiplying the result by 100. If the answer is more than the percentage which will require reporting to management, the variance is **significant**.

EXAMPLE: Identifying significant variances

Management has decided that any variance of **more than 2%** of the budgeted income or cost is significant, and will need to be reported. The next page shows you how this works.

	Budget £	**Actual £**	**Variance £**	**Variance %**	**Significant**
Income	200,000	198,500	1,500	0.75	
Direct materials	25,300	24,900	400	1.58	
Direct labour	48,600	49,700	1,100	2.26	✔
Production overheads	71,400	72,000	600	0.84	
Administration overheads	23,200	22,900	300	1.29	
Selling and distribution overheads	15,900	17,000	1,100	6.92	✔

Note that the direct labour variance is (£1,100 ÷ £48,600) x 100 = 2.26% of the budget amount, and so **is significant**.

But also note that the direct materials variance is (£400 ÷ £25,300) x 100 = 1.58% of the budget amount. As this is less than 2% this variance is **not significant**.

Also note that both an adverse variance and a favourable variance can be significant and need reporting.

14 Reporting

the need to report significant variances
In the last section we looked at performance reports that included significant variances. These are variances that need to be brought to the attention of a relevant manager for review or investigation. In this section we will look at which manager is the best person to approach for this sort of reporting.

the right manager
You will need to remember the various **functional areas** within a typical organisation, the **cost areas** they involve and the **appropriate manager** to report to. The main functional areas and the managers in charge of them are as follows.

production	administration	sales & distribution	finance
production manager	administration manager	sales manager distribution manager	finance manager company accountant

finding the right manager

Finding the right manager will depend on the area of cost involved. You should study the table set out below and remember the managers responsible for each type of cost. In the end it should all come down to common sense.

cost	manager responsible for cost
direct materials	production manager/purchasing manager
direct labour	production manager/human resources manager
production overheads	production manager
administration overheads	administration manager
sales & distribution overheads	sales manager/distribution manager
financial overheads	finance manager/company accountant

15 Calculation tools – spreadsheets

Spreadsheets can be used to calculate and report costing data easily. The following illustration shows how a typical spreadsheet page looks and how columns, rows and cells are identified.

- Columns are identified by letters (A, B, C etc) across the top of the page
- Rows are identified by numbers (1, 2, 3 etc) down the left side of the page
- Cells are identified by the column and row which shows their location (eg B5)

	A	B	C	D	E
1					
2					
3					
4					
5		**Cell B5**			

using formulas

addition

using + sign eg =C3+D3+E3

or using SUM, brackets and colon
(to show start and end of range) eg =SUM(C3:E3)

subtraction

using - sign eg =C3-D3

multiplication

using * sign to mean x eg =C3*D3

division

using / to mean ÷ eg =C3/D3

example – using addition and subtraction

The following spreadsheet shows the budgeted and actual data and variances.

Note how formulas have been used to calculate the content of some cells, and make sure that you can see how they work. Here we have made sure that favourable variances show as positive amounts, and adverse variances result in negative variances by using different orders of data within the formulas.

	A	B	C	D	E
1		Budget £	Actual £	Variance £	A / F
2	Income	150,000	152,000	=C2-B2	F
3	Direct materials	35,000	36,400	=B3-C3	A
4	Direct labour	42,500	40,900	=B4-C4	F
5	Overheads	58,000	60,000	=B5-C5	A
6	Total costs	=SUM(B3:B5)	=SUM(C3:C5)	=B6-C6	A
7	Profit	=B2-B6	=C2-C6	=C7-B7	F

Other formulas could be used to obtain the same results.

formatting

Make sure that you can apply the following processes to the contents of cells. Some processes have alternative ways that they can be implemented.

- thousand separators
- decimal places
- percentages
- accounting (e.g. £ sign and 2 decimal places)
- bold
- italics
- underline
- borders
- colour fill
- text size
- wrap text
- merge
- copy and paste
- insert rows and columns

16 Memory aids

KEEPING YOUR MEMORY FIT

The human brain is an odd organ – you can remember the most useless facts, but when it comes to complex matters such as accounting procedures the mind can go completely blank. But it is possible to train your brain.

At the beginning of this Guide there are some revision tips which suggest that you can study effectively and recall information by . . .

- **Observing**, *ie remembering what information looks like on the page, using diagrams, lists, mind-maps and colour coding. Memory is very visual.*

- **Writing** *information down, using flash cards, post-it notes, notes on a phone. It is the actual process of writing which helps to fix the information in the brain.*

- **Learning** *by regularly going through your course notes and text books. Find a 'study buddy' in your class (or online) to teach and test each other as the course progresses.*

- ***Chill out*** *when you get tired. Give your brain a chance to recover. Get some exercise and fresh air, work out. In the ancient world there was the saying that a fit body was usually home to a fit mind.*

- ***Treats*** *– promise yourself rewards when you have finished studying – meet friends, eat chocolate, have a drink, listen to music.*

exam preparation

- ***Practice, practice, practice*** *when preparing for your assessment.*
  Practice the questions and assessments in the Osborne Books workbooks.
  Practice the free online assessments on the Osborne Books website:
  Log on to www.osbornebooks.co.uk/elearning

some aids to memory

On the next few pages are blank spaces for you to set out ways of remembering many of the classifications of cost and inventory valuation methods.

elements of cost

Use the table below to provide examples of two types of manufacturing business and examples of their costs, classified into the elements of materials, labour and expenses.

business	materials	labour	expenses

nature of costs

Use the table below to think of a manufacturing business (eg a chocolate factory) and give examples of its direct and indirect costs for materials, labour and expenses.

Name of business:		
	Direct	**Indirect**
Materials		
Labour		
Expenses		

principles of costing wise guide – memory aids

cost behaviour

Use the table below to explain how different types of cost (fixed, variable and semi-variable) behave when the output of a manufacturing company doubles.

type of cost	how it behaves if output doubles
fixed costs	
variable costs	
semi-variable costs	

FIFO, LIFO and AVCO – valuation methods

Use the table below to state the methods of inventory valuation (ie which purchase prices are used) to value issues out of stores and inventory left in the stores.

method	issue from stores	inventory left in stores
FIFO		
LIFO		
AVCO		

index

Absorption of overheads, 26-29
    direct labour hours method, 28
    machine hours method, 29
    units of output method, 27
AVCO, 46-47
    valuation using table, 54-55

Bonus, 66
Budgets, 68-71
Buffer stock, 56

Calculation tools, 74-77
Coding, 22-25
Cost behaviour, 30-35
    calculations, 36-39
Cost centre, 23
Cost of goods manufactured, 59,61

Cost of goods sold, 59,62
Costing, 6
Costs
    direct, 12-17
    elements, 8-11
    expenses, 8-11,14
    fixed, 30-31, 34-35
    functional, 18-21
    indirect, 12-17
    labour, 8-11,14
    materials, 8-11,14
    nature of, 12-17
    non-production, 18-21
    production, 18-19,21
    semi-variable, 30,33-35
    variable, 30,32,34-35
Direct costs, 12-17,59-60

Elements of cost, 8-11

FIFO, 42-43
    valuation using table, 50-51
Financial accounting, 7
Fixed costs, 30-31, 34-35
Formatting, 77
Formulas, 75
Functional areas, 72

Indirect costs, 12-17
Inventory buffer, 56
Inventory control policy, 56
Inventory valuation, 40-55
    effects of price change, 49
    features of FIFO, LIFO & AVCO, 48
Investment centre, 23

Labour payments, 64-67
    bonus, 66
    cost behaviour, 67
    implications, 67
    overtime, 65
    piecework, 67
    time rate, 64-66
Lead time, 56
LIFO, 44-45
    valuation using table, 52-53

Management accounting, 7
Managing materials inventory, 56-57
Manufacturing accounts, 58-63
Manufacturing costs, 59, 61

Nature of costs, 12-17
Non-production costs, 18-21

Overhead absorption rate (OAR), 26-29
Overtime, 65

Performance report, 69
Piecework, 67
Prime cost, 63
Production costs, 18-19,21
Profit centre, 23

Re-order level, 57
Re-order quantity, 57
Reporting, 72-73
Responsible manager, 73

Semi-variable costs, 30,33-35
Spreadsheets, 74-77

Time rate, 64-66
Variable costs, 30,32,34-35
Variances, 68-71
    significant, 70-71